The Tudors

Written by Sally Hewitt

First published in 2006 by Franklin Watts
338 Euston Road, London NW1 3BH

Franklin Watts Australia
Hachette Children's Books
Level 17/207 Kent Street, Sydney NSW 2000

Copyright © Franklin Watts 2006

Editor: Rachel Tonkin
Designers: Rachel Hamdi and Holly Mann
Picture researcher: Diana Morris
Craft models made by: Rachel Tonkin

Picture credits:
ARPL/Topfoto: 15t, 18; © Pauline Baynes/Bridgeman Art
Library: 23t; Bettmann/Corbis: 22cr, 23b; Robert Estall/Corbis:
16b; Fotomas/Topfoto: 22cl; HIP/Topfoto: 8t, 25t; Longleat
House, Wiltshire, UK/Bridgeman Art Library: 12b; Musée du
Château de Versailles /Dagli Orti/Art Archive: 24; PA/Topfoto:
11t; Picturepoint/Topfoto: 14, 20b, 21t; Private
Collection/Bridgeman Art Library: 16t; PRO/HIP/Topfoto: 19t;
Roger-Viollet/Topfoto: 9t; R. Sheridan/Ancient Art &
Architecture Collection: endpapers, 6b; Topfoto: 10;
UPP/Topfoto: 20t; Woodmansterne/Topfoto: front cover t, 6t;
Adam Woolfitt/Corbis: 12t.

All other images: Steve Shott

With thanks to our model Reanne Khokhar

Every attempt has been made to clear copyright.
Should there be any inadvertent omission please
apply to the publisher for rectification.

A CIP catalogue record for this book
is available from the British Library

ISBN-10: 0 7496 6503 3
ISBN-13: 978 0 7496 6503 6

Dewey Classification: 942.05

Printed in China

Contents

The Tudors

Five Tudor kings and queens ruled England for 118 years from 1485 to 1603.

Wars of the Roses

Between 1455 and 1485, two families, called the House of York and the House of Lancaster, fought for the throne of England.

Their family **emblems** were roses: a red rose for Lancaster and a white rose for York. The fight for the throne became known as the Wars of the Roses.

The rose window at York Minster marks the joining of the two families and the beginning of Tudor rule.

The Tudor Rose was used to decorate everyday items, such as this cushion.

Tudor Rose

In 1485, Henry Tudor, of the House of Lancaster, defeated King Richard III and became King Henry VII. He married Elizabeth of York and combined the two roses to make a new emblem – the Tudor rose.

Make a stained-glass rose window

▶ 1 Draw round a dinner plate on thin black paper and cut out the circle. Fold it in half, then in half again, and then repeat.

▶ 2 Copy these shapes onto the folded paper. Ask an adult to help you cut them out. Open out the circle.

▶ 3 Stick bright-coloured tissue paper over the holes on one side.

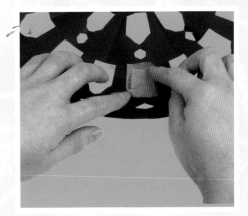

▶ 4 Make a Tudor rose to go in the centre with gold, white and red paper. Add four green leaves around the edge.

Henry VIII

Henry VIII became king when he was only 17 after the death of his father, Henry VII.

Henry VIII loved hunting, sport and rich banquets. He wanted to be seen as a powerful king in Europe as well as at home. He longed for a son and **heir** to the throne. Henry VIII is famous for having married six times.

In this famous portrait by Hans Holbein, Henry VIII (aged 49) is dressed in expensive clothes and jewels. He looks rich and powerful.

The six wives of Henry VIII

Catherine of Aragon
Henry's first wife was Catherine of Aragon who had six children. Five died young and only one daughter, Mary, survived. Henry **divorced** Catherine so he could marry Anne Boleyn.

Anne Boleyn
Anne Boleyn had a daughter, Elizabeth, but no son. Henry believed she had been **unfaithful** and she was **executed**.

Jane Seymour
Jane Seymour died after giving birth to a son, Edward, who became King Edward VI.

Anne of Cleves

Anne of Cleves was a German princess. Henry divorced her after only six months of marriage.

Catherine Howard

Catherine Howard was 30 years younger than Henry when they married. She was unfaithful to Henry and he ordered her to be executed.

Catherine Parr was Henry's sixth wife.

Catherine Parr

Catherine Parr looked after Henry and his three children until he died in 1543.

Make a portrait of Henry VIII

▶ 1 Collect materials such as lace, ribbon, fur, feathers, sequins, beads and gold or silver ribbon.

▶ 2 Copy this outline of Henry VIII onto a piece of A3 card.

▶ 3 Paint his face and the background. Finish your portrait using collage materials. Make the king look as rich and powerful as you can.

Life at court

Henry VIII's **court** was wherever he was living at the time. It could be at any of his many palaces. He travelled between palaces with his **courtiers** and servants and stayed for about three months before moving on.

Foreign visitors

To show how powerful he was, Henry entertained important people from foreign countries. He impressed his visitors with huge feasts, sport, music, dance and poetry.

Hampton Court was one of Henry VIII's favourite palaces.

Hampton Court Palace

Hampton Court was one of Henry's six London palaces. It had three big kitchens where meals for as many as 1,000 people were cooked. Rich tapestries and grand portraits hung on the walls.

Palace gardens

Guests could stroll in the beautiful gardens of his palaces among fountains and flowerbeds. They might even get lost in a maze. Hedge mazes were popular in Tudor gardens. You had to find your way along the paths to the centre – then out again!

The maze at Hampton Court was designed in the style of a Tudor maze.

Design a maze

▶ 1 Roll out long sausages of green modelling clay. Flatten them so they stand up like hedges.

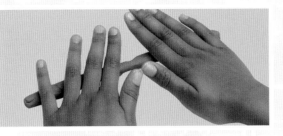

▶ 2 Paint a piece of cardboard green. Lay out the modelling clay to form a maze. Smooth out the joins in the hedges.

▶ 3 See if your friends can find their way to the centre of your maze.

Tudor homes

Only the royal family and **nobles** lived in palaces and grand houses.

Middle-class Tudors, such as farmers, doctors and **lawyers**, lived comfortably. But life could be hard for servants and labourers who were often very poor.

This is what the inside of a Tudor house would have looked like.

Furniture

An ordinary Tudor home would have just a few pieces of furniture, usually made of wood, and useful things such as bedding, pots and tools.

A painting of a wealthy Tudor family.

Inventories

An inventory is a list of someone's belongings. People made inventories to record what they owned. Inventories tell us interesting things about them.

When he died, Edward Jaxson owned 1 broken table, 2 old carpenter's chairs, 3 mattresses and 30 acres of corn. So we know that he owned land in the country but he wasn't rich.

Make an inventory

Margery Wren owned 10 featherbeds, 20 pairs of linen sheets, 48 bowls, many cows, sheep and pigs, 2 ploughs, and a money chest.

▶ What do her belongings tell you about her?

▶ Make an inventory of the things in your bedroom.

If someone found it in 500 years' time, what would they learn about you?

1 bed

1 desk

2 chairs

1 chest of drawers

2 lamps

1 rug

Tudor London

Tudor London was a busy city and port. Ships sailed up and down the River Thames bringing **goods** from abroad. Rich **merchants** lived in large houses but many of the streets were crowded and smelly. Rubbish was thrown out onto the streets and into the river as there was nowhere to put it.

Plague

Rats with fleas scurried from house to house. Drinking water was dirty. Many people died of the **plague** in Tudor London as disease spread quickly.

People carried sweet-smelling pomanders of herbs and spices through the stinking London streets to protect them from the awful smell and disease.

This is what the busy River Thames would have looked like in Tudor times.

A painting of the Tower of London.

The Tower of London was a prison as well as a palace. Traitors who plotted against the king or queen were executed there.

Make a pomander

▶ **1** Cut a square of light cloth such as muslin, 20cm x 20cm.

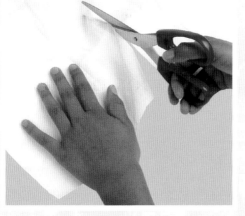

▶ **2** Collect dried petals of scented flowers such as roses, jasmine and lavender. You will also need slivers of lemon and orange peel and some herbs and spices.

▶ **3** Put a handful of dried petals on the square of cloth. Add two bay leaves, a pinch of rosemary, a few cloves and the slices of peel.

▶ **4** Gather the corners of the cloth together and twist in the middle. Secure with a length of ribbon.

Street life

There were no police on the Tudor streets to protect people. Rich people had to guard their money as **pickpockets** lay in wait. It was against the law to beg but people often did.

A beggar being chased out of town.

Homes for the poor

Rich people were expected to give alms to the deserving poor, such as the old or sick. **Almshouses** were built to give poor people somewhere to live.

Street sellers and entertainment

Jesters, jugglers and **minstrels** could earn money by entertaining the crowds at festivals and even public executions.

The cries of street sellers advertised hot pies, baked meats and apples, bread, fruit and fresh fish for sale.

A Tudor almshouse in Oxfordshire.

Make a jester's hat

▶ **1** Make four copies of the shape below on paper about the size of this page; use two different colours. Make two copies in each colour.

▶ **3** Glue the points of the hat together at the very ends.

▶ **4** Add bells, pom-poms or whatever you have to the points of the hat. Now it's ready to wear!

▶ **2** Tape the sides together, as shown below. Then tape the ends so that it fits around your head.

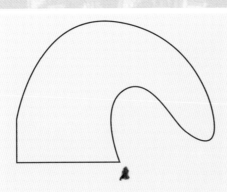

Elizabeth I

Elizabeth I's **reign** lasted for 45 years and is sometimes called a 'golden age'. She was popular with her people and never married. She said she was married to 'the Kingdom of England'. During this time, England became strong and powerful.

Elizabeth made sure that all paintings of her made her look powerful, rich and attractive.

Plots

Many **plots** were made to overthrow Elizabeth. She had to be strong and **ruthless** to hold onto power. Her cousin, Mary Queen of Scots, plotted against her and Elizabeth was forced to execute her.

The Great Seal

The Great Seal was stamped onto letters and documents to prove they had the royal 'seal of approval'. Elizabeth's seal showed her crowned and holding an **orb and sceptre**.

On this seal, Elizabeth is shown riding a horse across a field.

Design and make a seal

Design your own seal. Think about what you want to show on it and why.

▶ 1 Plan your design in pencil in a circle on paper – about 6cm in diameter. Make a cylinder of air-hardening clay in the same diameter.

▶ 2 Using another piece of clay, cut out the shapes for your design. Moisten the clay with water and stick the shapes onto the cylinder.

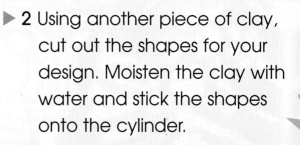

▶ 3 Leave the clay to dry. Then, stamp your seal into a blob of Plasticine to leave the impression on it.

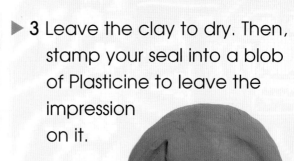

Exploration

During Tudor times, explorers sailed the oceans to discover new lands. They returned from Asia and North America with silks, spices, tobacco, pineapples, tomatoes and potatoes – fruit and vegetables that had never been seen in England before.

Drake would have sailed in a ship like this.

Danger at sea

Sailors were often in danger from storms, hunger and thirst, disease and pirates. Sir Francis Drake became rich by attacking Spanish ships and robbing them of gold and goods. He was also the first Englishman to sail round the world. It took him four years.

Sir Walter Raleigh was a successful sailor.

Sir Walter Raleigh

Sir Walter Raleigh sailed to North America. He claimed land there for England.

Sailors looked out for the Pole Star to help them navigate their way round the world. It is always in the North.

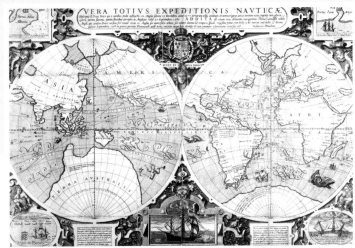

This map of the world was used by Sir Francis Drake.

Make a star map

▶ **1** Draw around a dinner plate on some black card and cut out. Copy the stars shown below onto the card in pencil.

▶ **3** Stick silver stars on the brightest stars. Make a silver blob on less bright stars.

Pole Star

Cassiopeia

Ursa Major

Aries

Orion

▶ **4** On a bright night, look at the stars and see if you can find the stars on your map. You can also look at websites to see more stars: www.bbc.co.uk/science/space/myspace/

▶ **2** Join the stars in each constellation with a silver pen line.

Tudor childhood

Boys from wealthy homes went to school or were taught at home. Girls learnt to be good wives and housekeepers. Village boys could go to their local **'Petty' school** and learn to read and write. Some went on to **grammar schools**.

This engraving shows a Tudor classroom.

A short childhood

Poor children often had to work to bring in money for their families. Between the ages of 7 and 9, boys began to learn a trade and girls became servants. Children in the countryside worked in the fields. Girls could marry when they were only 12 years old.

Children learnt to read from a horn book made from very thin horn-covered paper.

Toys and games

Only rich children had well-made toys. Poorer children played together in the fields and streets. They made hoops, skittles and balls, and marbles from old barrels, rags, sticks, clay or whatever they could find.

Make and play skittles

▶ **1** Collect five small plastic bottles with screw-top lids. Decorate them with paint or coloured paper.

▶ **2** Put a little water in the bottles and screw on the lids. Make a ball with strips of rags – or cut a J-cloth into 20cm x 3cm strips.

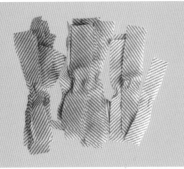

▶ **3** Use one strip to tie them tightly round the middle. Spread out the strips to make a ball.

▶ **4** Arrange the skittles in a triangle. Take it in turns with your friends to knock them down with the rag ball.

Food

Tudor kings and queens impressed their foreign guests with expensive banquets. Wild boar, deer, beef, lamb, fish and all kinds of birds including swans and peacocks were served. Marzipan made from sugar, almonds and rose water was moulded into animals and flowers.

Christmas celebrations in Tudor times.

Everyday food

Ordinary people ate turnips, cabbage and beans. They ate bread at every meal. In the country they might catch rabbits, wild birds and fish to eat.

In the towns, street traders sold hot pies, sausages and baked apples.

This is the kitchen at Hampton Court Palace.

Keeping food fresh

In the past, it was difficult to keep food fresh. Meat was salted to stop it going bad. Fruit was made into jam and vegetables were pickled.

Curds

In Tudor times, curds were made from heating buttermilk (the liquid left over after making butter), and milk straight from the cow. When it thickened, it was strained, then cooled. Lemon and honey and thick cream were added to make lemon curd.

Ingredients

75g caster sugar
• rind and juice of 1 large lemon
• 2 large eggs
• 50g unsalted butter

Make modern lemon curd

Ask an adult to help you with this recipe.

▶ 1 Finely grate the lemon rind and put into a heavy-bottomed saucepan. Add the sugar and mix together.

▶ 2 Squeeze the lemon juice into a bowl and break in the eggs. Whisk them together and pour the mixture over the sugar.

▶ 3 Cut the butter into small pieces and add to the mixture. Stir over a low heat for about 20 minutes until the lemon curd is thick and smooth.

▶ 4 You can have your lemon curd on toast or bake it in some pastry cases to make lemon curd tarts.

Theatre

All over England, plays were performed by actors in barns and courtyard inns, and in the halls of great houses and universities. In Tudor London, there were theatres such as the Swan, the Rose and the Globe. Audiences paid a penny to stand in the open air to see a play or paid more for a seat in the gallery.

Acting

Actors wore Tudor clothes whatever the play. Women were not allowed to perform so boys played women's roles. Scenery and **props** were very simple.

William Shakespeare

William Shakespeare wrote popular plays that are still performed in theatres today.

A painting of Shakespeare, aged 34.

The original Globe theatre opened in 1598. Many of Shakespeare's plays were performed there.

In 1997, the Globe theatre was rebuilt as it would have been in Tudor times.

Make a model of the Globe theatre

▶ 1 You need a piece of cream A3 card. Fold down 3.5cm at the top and at the bottom. Snip from the edge to the folds 10cm in from the side – in 4 places – as shown below.

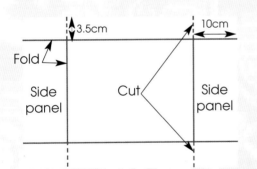

▶ 2 Draw or paint on the galleries and the audience on the side panels. Bend the card round and stick the card where you cut it in place. Stick snipped art straws along the top fold to make the thatched roof.

▶ 3 Paint a small box for the stage. Fold a rectangle of card 15cm x 6cm and stick on snipped art straws for the stage canopy. Attach the canopy to the stage using art straws as pillars.

Glossary

Almshouses
Houses built to give poor people somewhere to live.

Court
The place where a king or queen lived together with his or her officials.

Courtiers
Someone who attended the king or queen's court.

Divorce
To end a marriage legally.

Emblem
A symbol or badge.

Execute
To kill someone as a punishment.

Goods
Things that are bought and sold.

Grammar schools
A secondary school.

Heir
The person who will become king or queen when the existing king or queen dies.

Jester
Someone who entertained people, often at the royal court.

Lawyer
Someone who is an expert in the law and helps people with legal matters.

Merchant
A person who buys and sells things.

Minstrel
A musician who travelled round the country.

Nobles
Someone from the upper classes, usually owning a lot of land.

Orb and sceptre

An orb was a globe with a cross on top. A sceptre was a long stick. These were both used by a king or queen as symbols of power.

Petty school

A school where children were taught at the house of a well-educated woman. Children were taught to read and write, and how to behave.

Pickpocket

Someone who steals things from people's pockets.

Plague

A dangerous illness that spread by flea bites. The fleas lived on rats. The plague killed thousands of people in Tudor times.

Plot

A secret plan.

Props

Things used in a play

Reign

The time when someone is king or queen.

Ruthless

Cruel and having no pity.

Unfaithful

To have a relationship with someone you are not married to.

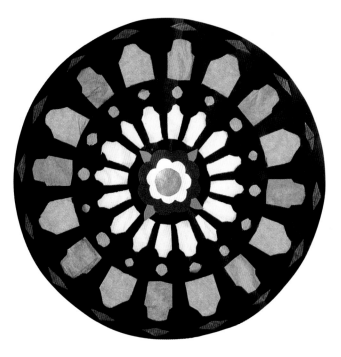

Index